STARK LIBRARY  NOV - - 2022

DISCARD

My First Time
Getting a New Baby

by Jeri Cipriano

Red Chair Press   Egremont, Massachusetts

Look! Books are produced and published by Red Chair Press:
Red Chair Press LLC PO Box 333 South Egremont, MA 01258-0333

 FREE Educator Guides at www.redchairpress.com/free-resources

Publisher's Cataloging-In-Publication Data

Names: Cipriano, Jeri, author.

Title: Getting a new baby / by Jeri Cipriano.

Description: Egremont, Massachusetts : Red Chair Press, [2021] | Series: Look! books. My first time | Includes index and a list of resources for further reading. | Interest age level: 005-008. | Summary: "When a new baby comes home to a family, it means huge changes in everyone's life. A new baby brother or sister will need lots of attention from Mom and Dad. That's where you come in, discover some of the things you can do to help out and learn more about what will happen at home"--Provided by publisher.

Identifiers: ISBN 9781643710938 (RLB hardcover) | ISBN 9781643710990 (softcover) | ISBN 9781643711058 (ebook)

Subjects: LCSH: Infants--Care--Juvenile literature. | Infants--Family relationships--Juvenile literature. | CYAC: Babies--Care.

Classification: LCC HQ774 .C56 2021 (print) | LCC HQ774 (ebook) | DDC 649.122--dc23

LCCN: 2020948758

Copyright © 2022 Red Chair Press LLC
RED CHAIR PRESS, the RED CHAIR and associated logos are registered trademarks of Red Chair Press LLC.

All rights reserved. No part of this book may be reproduced, stored in an information or retrieval system, or transmitted in any form by any means, electronic, mechanical including photocopying, recording, or otherwise without the prior written permission from the Publisher. For permissions, contact info@redchairpress.com

Photo credits: iStock; P.24: Nick Magliato

Printed in United States of America
0421 1P CGF21

Table of Contents

A New Baby 4

As Babies Grow 6

Welcome, Baby! 10

Smiles and Laughs 12

Best Buddies 14

What Do You Know? 16

You Are Special 18

The Future is Now 20

Words to Know 23

Learn More at the Library 23

Index 24

About the Author 24

A New Baby

Is your family expecting a new baby? When you were born, everyone made a big fuss. You can't remember that. So you may not know what to expect.

One thing is sure. You may not be able to sit on your mother's lap for long.

As Babies Grow

A baby will grow inside your mother for nine months. By the time it is ready to be born, your mom may look like she swallowed a big balloon!

Good to Know

Talk to the baby while it is still in mommy's belly. The baby will know your voice when it is born!

Knock, Knock—Who's There?

 **5 weeks:** The baby looks like a **tadpole** with a tail. Its heart starts to beat.

 **6 weeks:** The baby's nose, mouth, and ears are starting to grow. It is the size of a lentil.

 **10 weeks:** Tiny arms and legs are growing. Fingernails are growing, too.

 **11 weeks:** Baby kicks and stretches— even hiccups!

 **14 weeks:** Baby is the size of a lemon.

 **19 weeks:** Baby can hear your voice! You can sing and talk to the baby!

22 weeks: Baby's lips and eyebrows are forming.

24 weeks: Baby is the size of an ear of corn.

27 weeks: Baby sleeps and wakes on a **regular schedule**.

28 weeks: Baby's eyesight is developing. Eyelashes are growing in.

31 weeks: Baby can turn its head from side to side.

39 weeks: Baby is complete. It is putting on weight.

40 weeks: Baby is getting ready to meet the family.

Welcome, Baby!

When babies are born, they are helpless. They weigh around 5 to 8 pounds. Their heads are about 13 inches around.

> New babies cannot hold their heads up on their own. Be sure to support the baby's head.

Babies Eat, Sleep, and Cry

Babies eat and sleep a lot. They gain one ounce every day for the first month.

What Can You Do?

Not much. You can speak softly to the baby. Pat the baby's back. It knows you. You are helping to make the baby feel safe.

Good to Know

All babies' eyes are blue at birth. The color changes and darkens as babies grow.

Smiles and Laughs

Babies smile and laugh when they are six months old.

Here's where YOU come in. Play "peek-a-boo." Show the baby how to clap its hands.

Oh, Happy Day!
Babies learn to talk around one year old. They **crawl** and start to walk. Play music. Sing songs. Dance to the music. See if the little one copies you.

Best Buddies

You two are becoming buddies. Brothers and sisters may stay close their whole lives!

Babies Want to Learn

Babies are born wanting to learn. They can learn by watching their older sister or brother.

Babies want to do what you do. You can tie your shoes. You can draw with crayons. You can paint.

You can do a lot of things. You can sing. You can dance. You can skip. You can ride a bike.

Little brothers or sisters think older **siblings** can do everything. They want to be just like you.

What Do You Know?

Teach the little one to be kind, just like you.

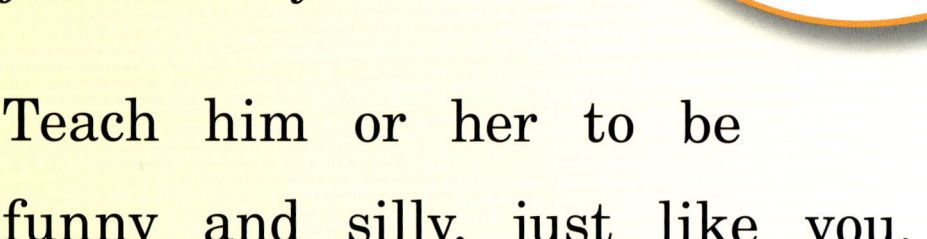

Teach him or her to be fair, just like you.

Teach him or her to be funny and silly, just like you.

You can be his role model.

You Are Special

Pass on what you know to the little one. Then *both* of you will make your family proud.

Ask your folks what they love about you. Tell your family what you love about them. What do you like doing together?

What can *everyone*, including baby, do together?

The Future is Now

You and your new baby will spend years and years together. You will grow up together.

What do you "see" yourselves doing together? Draw the story you "see" in your mind.

Words to Know

crawl: move forward on hands and knees

regular: usual or typical

schedule: certain times that things take place

sibling: a brother or a sister

tadpole: the early stage of a frog when it lives in water and doesn't have legs for walking on land

Learn More at the Library

Check out these books to learn more.

Guillain, Charlotte. *A New Brother or Sister.* Heinemann-Raintree, 2011.

Sears RN, Martha and Sears MD, William. *Baby on the Way.* Little Brown Books, 2001.

Index

babies' eyes 11
mommy's belly 6
role model 16

About the Author

Jeri Cipriano enjoys writing for children of all ages. She loves to learn new things she can share with others.